Keeping The Chaff And The Wheat

Marine Cornuet

Copyright©2018 Marine Cornuet
All Rights Reserved

Published by Unsolicited Press
Portland, Oregon
www.unsolicitedpress.com

No part of this book may be reproduced or transmitted in any form or by any means without written permission from the publisher or author.

Printed in the United States of America.

Attention schools and businesses: for discounted copies on large orders, please contact the publisher directly.

ISBN: 978-1-947021-64-8

Keeping The Chaff And The Wheat

CONTENTS

Villagers	9
I.	11
To Grandmothers	12
Noel	14
From Nine to Eight	16
Opinel	18
The Keeping	20
II.	23
After A Big Family Meal	24
Belote	31
III.	32
Visiting Grandma	33
Techniques	36
Keeping the Chaff and the Wheat	37
Ode to Hot Water	38
Sisters Dream	39
IV.	40
They come on vacation	41
Whirlpool	43
Satellite	44
Prunes	46
Dune	48
V.	50
Acknowledgements	57
About The Author	58

Keeping The Chaff And The Wheat

VILLAGERS

There's a harshness
    something I know
is ours   forever villagers
even when we've walked miles
to get crammed with others
    there's a harshness
that comes straight from the blood
from times untamed   unkind
by necessity   a rope stretching
between our veins   dreamcaught
something birds brought
to the next nest and tied
to their offsprings' legs
something their parents did
    something without thinking
and it made them feel safe
like a trussed-up partridge

My cousin killed a dove for me
it wasn't a metaphor
    with a single finger
    he said *come* to the bird
he needed to show me
how much undoing
could be inflicted
with the fifth of a hand
he laughed but I know

he felt like crying   in the margins
there's a harshness
that takes it all at the end
of the day at the end of the thickest night
where there's no winners
no answers   it's the last joke we have
    we click
our tongues on the roof
of our fears and hang on tight
to the harshness
    it's real
        this rope
curling around our thighs
as if it were justice
the end to loose ends
the faith we can walk
head first through every mess
we'll get hurt but hurting
is just life drawing
the outline of itself
    our fingers are striped
from pulling this rope
we can tie it pretty well
nice and tight around ourselves

I.

Watch   in the river bed
how parts are slowly set
     cogs askew   in mouths
we have time here
to re-open and ask
     unroll the storyline

TO GRANDMOTHERS

One traveled squeezed
between two wars
    chest crusted and hands
blue at seventeen

    red mute son
already screwed to the hip
    bent to tear
potatoes off a field

The other stayed
with dying in-laws
    joints flat
from kneeler practice

    heart cupped
to receive girls
after they scraped
their wombs clean

In my blood
    my grandmothers
pushed two yokes full
of clenched teeth

    the way women
keep carrying children

and stories they don't always
get to tell

    the way they roll
stones of rage and wit
up and over
the century's angry hills

NOEL

Under slapped dirt
once fresh   of the barn
    a slaughter of boars

one for each Christmas
    and frozen oranges
finally sit in open palms

Blow the candles
    little darlings
on the clammy table cloth

A newborn fusses
    - the seventh -
    tiny nostrils eager
for the scent of meat broth

        In between wails
        brews a silence
        the future hunter's precious doubt

        and under nails
        the size of dew drops
        callous fingers begin to sprout

Look out the window
    and make a wish

above a forest of braids

Stick your small hand
    into the snow
search for the treasure you left

While father snores and mother
moans   while brothers
and sisters roll their heads

a girl in sheets   all bones
and cheeks   nibbles then chews
on orange peels

FROM NINE TO EIGHT

He sat
on his siblings' shoulders
little ivy
forever green

I saw his tongue
     serpent sweet
and his folded
paper crown

His slender cheek
resting on my mother's
as they piggybacked
on weeded concrete

carousing
     lolloping
          falling
failing to forget

A stone for a name
an ingrained pebble
     no she wasn't to blame
        Ghost brother never stopped

clutching   little ivy
always seen

on his siblings' faces
    They've carried

his lush green
    to the edge
    to the creases
wrinkles and bottles

always guessing
in the mirror
on the blue shores
beneath the eyes

of their children
    inevitable
    There   he still hangs
        refusing to turn to grey

OPINEL

If you have a knife   you have everything
my uncle says

Him and his brothers   his sons
and his nephews pull out of their pockets
the mark of manhood
at each meal

An Opinel is a sharp sunflower:
it unfolds when a plate appears
and is crumpled back into darkness
when the meal is done
        The men in my family cut
and slice in silence   then sweetly
rinse and pat their blades
dry

An Opinel is a durable tool
that if cared for properly   brings
you food and safety   *I gutted*
this boar with mine
        my uncle continues

He offered a knife to his wife
as a wedding gift   She knows
how to prepare excellent deer
with the soft potatoes they grow

    flat parsley and garlic   also
from their small plot

The only way to say
I love you   with a knife
    in your pocket
is to kill game
and carry it home
for dinner

THE KEEPING

Front gate flaky
    white paint high
so high cause
a dog could fly and stretched
his stomach open once
    wild friend my younger uncle said
adding and painting a meter
of wire fencing   shaking
his pollen curls in a dawn golden
    wheat dust roaring
in the field far beyond

There's a memory
of each and every thing
stuck in rocks walls hulls piles of straw
    wallpapered under wallpaper
over large wooden beams
under wood stoves
over fresh fences
under whole sentences
kept between closed shutters
inside cat bags thrown in rivers
    in resting thoughts
chiming over cold beds
repeating stories   heads shaking
to repeat stories as jokes
around tables over dirt roads

    under curves under earth
over hands lit by green beans
    over pulp polished by motor grease

He's undoing
another whole moped
scattering parts   harvesting
what is needed to ride again
face full of wildflowers
combusting in silence
    flowers don't speak
don't reveal how
flowers collapse fold harden
rocks drop in a garden
and still there is a keeping
somewhere of it all

II.

Like a bride I let go
of the dream
that everything will be right
and I step through
all this water
words are streams
     that could empty
us out

AFTER A BIG FAMILY MEAL

A.
Today we talk
      about weather   work
cousins   kids   aches
      with drama voices flare
while tragic never speaks

there's still this red
      pacing around as if
I'm not sure it's a color
      warm and dilating
thrust too fast
      lurking while
pretending everything
      was said
across the endless table
      pickled   canned
from some year's harvest
      kept forever
a lifetime

Has it been tamed
      or will it cover
our faces
      and when we look
at our hands

Solid in the cold
   dogs anticipate
the hunt
   nudging our thighs
tender hunger
   unaware in their hutches
rabbits sniff
   outside and loved
in opposite ways
   I can't stand it
it's not in vain
   they call me city kid

There's no light here
   or no eyes just
the feeling of
   an undecided color

butcher cut blast
born faster monster guts
mouth spill throat past
ooze collapse shake crash
blade broken jaws slashed
ankles teeth skinned and raw

Turn on the lights
   it's too red and
no answer I know
   it's packed in here

and we just can't
            name it
we can only
            eat it
prepared for days
            in the kitchen
brown tiles and filled
            molars sucking
on cigarettes
            love is all
in the cooking
            where else
where else is it
            held in

Glare of the screen
            it's overcast
it always is
            and still we come
familiar sitting
            after the feast
close enough
            smelling like meat
dogs sleep
            in the veranda
our hands are knots
            as we finally stand
to leave doubts
            and crumbs

we'll once again
        brush off

B.
Dip in moonshine
        a big man's lips
crack open wide
        white lightning try
apple pear or prune stark
        against the dark
of supertight coffee
        how do we move
from here
        we're a monster
full of arms
        on the upside
of the sun
        sweet liquor
makes bodies run
        dishes fly
from porch to dim
        kitchen dirt white
on brown and swift
        pink of wet sponge
like a wink
        in an aunt's eye
we roll around full
        of six types of meat
extinguished by hands

       that wiped grease
on paper napkins

       three dogs wrestle
over-excitedly
       in the yard I see
rabbits huddle
       in their hutches
their time goes on
       at least til evening

the newest generation
       occupies the sofa
attention split between screen
       and comic strips
it's always like that
       white lightning
a possibility
       it's a laugh it's a joke
echoing from the veranda
       a fist pounding
onto checkered
       plastic cloth
a row of kids pinching
       flesh to feel
some sort of touch
       or getting crisp
in the yard
       over grass and cigarettes

    a mother rubs
           her child's bruise
and pats
           the back of her siblings

mémère will be alright
           remember that water fight
on your 50th birthday
           we cut sunflowers and cast
their shine in big buckets
           even the barn was full of dancing

Younger kids doze
           and whine
and chuckle
           while parents exchange
murmurs and recipes
           my mother utters
a few questions
           who keeps taking
pépère's old things
           what are doctors
really saying and when
           do our men
 begin breaking
           whose fault
whose fault is it
           was it mine
no one ever

        wants to answer
I also need
        to crack the code
I also forget
        to speak the truth
but today
        throats are full
no one will talk
        and unlocking
takes big luck
        and trust and
a special kind of asking

dogs are snoring
        like rugs in the veranda
my eyelids flutter
        I whisper to my sister
we're leaving
        as the whole room rises
we give kisses
        by the dozen
starlings fill the hallway
        and flee out
through the back door

BELOTE

stand up   open shout   signal
to your partner   gather fossils
of reddish nights   fire or not
we round   we still know one
another   the cheater
    the stubborn   the clown
       the luck-in-passing
          the challenger   the forgiving
sit again and again
in the evening
the same game

we stopped when age said

but my heart popped
when my aunt wrote
that they all sat   stood
    signaled   and shouted
       cheated   teamed up
gave up   won
over those same cards
on New Year's Day

III.

Watch as foreheads
    slide from right to left
left to right   no tugging
just a slow no   the children
come closer
to understanding

VISITING GRANDMA

We walk at first through the blindest night
set off on toes as we feel the breath
of hunting dogs at our ankles
bright dead eyes dot the field
this evening the sheep are sleeping outside

we hurry   the night is packed
with darkness and whimpers and footsteps
and now we run like there's a chill
like we're alone and a shape   faceless
is slipping   out of the barn

I see it   moving slowly   something someone
out to rip   our sisterly youth   on the outskirts
of the village   red ribbons stained
our hair   drenched   in a puddle of fresh
our limbs   our flesh   we leap   we fly

up the outdoor staircase   corrugated sheets
yell around our shoulders   I'm the eldest
     I let you go first   I push you upwards
we stumble   cold wood on our palms
splinters   sallow waves   endless slope

nails   scratching our hope   breaths
trapped in clouds   single lamp dangling
almost-rope hanging   at the very top

the key   enters the hole   our feet
quick like tiny flames   a click

you look back   you're always braver
I shoulder the door   propel you in
shut it too hard   its glass shivers
you grip the lace   pull the curtain
we wait

we wait in the unbearable blue   our mouths
silent   our ears so still   our hands locked
walls sinking   our brains rolling til
the clock   begins to show
a reasonable way to our hearts   we wait

til we remember
    this is where they used to sleep
every old night   our uncles or aunts
or someone   we look around
and through our search

we start to forget the night
open again   the drawers of time
to look at this photo of 1959   a young man
in uniform   peach-faced
gazing out of the cheap silver frame

we slide into the square of the bed
how did her brother   become so thick

we wonder   til our mother comes up
to feed the little wood stove
we nod as she asks   if all is well

TECHNIQUES

Us kids melt
      trying to overcome

          still struggling to weed
                out a level of freedom
          still sown with gaping need
          stamped with a hole
                that isn't ours to grieve

trying to become
      something else
          than someone's children
          than someone's held breath
      constantly halfway
          with a certain joy

incredibly anxious
      to be lost
      to lose
          when it's our turn
          to hold

KEEPING THE CHAFF AND THE WHEAT

My mother is the finest joker
we snicker   after she finds in her soup
a rough word   my grandmother
said on the phone   Oh how she shares it
eyebrows a sudden bridge   pout
and caged chin   the best caricature
in town   *stupid pig-headed* and we laugh
at knowing we are of the same wood   grumble
    noogie   rude   elated
at the thought   my mother taught
us to hide it well   Humor is laughing at
what you haven't got   when you ought
to have it   in our case chaff and wheat
have been separated   we're soft-spoken
but deep down   we know we lack
the smooth   the ease   we feign never
to have wanted   we know
that under strain or faced with
a mighty tough joke   we'll be coarse
and mean   all the same

ODE TO HOT WATER

Trickling between
shoulder blades
dissolving dirt and tension

transforming breaths
into clouds   a bunch
of dry sticks
      into a body

soothing the rage
of an uncontrollable child
- was it my sister

      or me? -
Hot water
     the peace

of muscles
     and of a turbulent mind

SISTERS DREAM

We'd call three times a week   we'd learn about
each other's days   of how they came and flew
from our blinking palms   we'd always know
how to ask   and catch and throw and sprout

Speaking low until the shout   our mouths
sweet like pears   words like friends and rivers
covered grooves   ransomless   hard givers
we'd rest   our blood tired from our growths

If and if   I'd tell you how I yearn
as I know you do too   we the tortoise
we the stuck in throats   we never learned

we the queens of awkward   we still return
to fill our missing years   we drip with poise
sometimes   and let our voices wrap the burn

IV.

I can feel it coming
    you say
and I freeze
this is why
I came down
    parasol ears
paralyzed

THEY COME ON VACATION

      we're all waiting for them
house clean   beds made   freezer full
      of ice cream   I act cool
their car pulls in   I wait the few minutes
      of pride to go out and greet them
awkwardness a first nature
      a full year has passed and
I'm afraid we've changed
      from my thirteen
to his fourteen   we take
      their bags   pack
their meats in the fridge
      start cooking and I wait
until dessert to ask my cousin
      if he'll still be sleeping
in my room
      how I hope we'll be talking
until the night buries
      the afternoon heat   hour
upon hour of asking
      until our faces stop sweating
and we'll crawl in our beds
      eyes making sense of shadows
shifting curtains swept
      by the fan's stubborn wing
sinking into sleep
      sinking into a future

we can only try to guess
        and this year I'm grateful
that we'll keep guessing
        just one last time
with luck we'll be swimming
        with all our words
into whatever we think
        is possible

WHIRLPOOL

the ultimate embrace
that of water   packed   pressed
pressing   kind on each pore of our skin
a deep hum saying
there is no need to swim
     we carry   and we are carried
in the current
we formed in the pool
     if we keep going
we'll be wrapped   hugged   moved
by all this liquid hope
     legs   arms   torso
wreathed and shipped
for another rotation
     trip around   our tiny galaxy
where I flip my head back
to laugh at the sun's big face
     taking a summer breath
before diving   completely
to see us run
     ahead of ourselves   we're all equal
     in slow motion
oh yes we're running
     on the most gleeful orbit
     ever   ever   ever

SATELLITE

We hold forbidden hands until cicadas die
from our wrong-doing   the television so low
we can barely follow the plot   and we couldn't care
less   our parents are siblings

We unhinge shields shell by shell   Our hair
wilts under a canopy of fans   You admonish
my lack of trust   I sing the song
    of your expansion   how moronic

One day your mind flies off a roof your lungs
open like marigolds singing their last song at dusk
    your brain glued to the moon too hard circling
    our planet still there yet gone you
        lovely   satellite

Insects scrape their sides in silence where gravity
does not apply   In your throat
    daily doses of asteroids are pressed
those palms I touched lie docile   flapping on your knees

like pale rubber pancakes   I visit you and wish
upon you eager rows of lavender   The type we crushed
between our fingers   to cover the smell
of the endless blunts traveling

from your mouth to mine   Smoke

for an early shrine   a tender fog to blur your words
    our summers   your spine   I didn't think
heat could ever sink where it used to leap

on the damp dirt beneath the evergreens
Your body reclines on the dry fragrant soil   or stretches
alone on the tired sofa   Clusters of half-thoughts
hover   A frozen mobile
                gently removed
                      from my grasp

PRUNES

chewing open-mouthed
laughter   tartness   tears
scaring ghosts in the chicken coop
scratching hay   hunting gossips
about the dead and the living
    all this til you'd whisper
      rolling eyes   almost green
        behind you, a snake!
two finches   racing above dirt
would tumble into high grass
    we'd spit all the pits
in the brisk behind the barn
    shooing away our respective siblings
triumphant   selfish   we seemed
stronger   our grandmother loved us
better   we fell and leapt and flew

today again   I caught you
    so high strung above the ward
smoke-wrapped   sortof talking
    you said you'd been prying
secrets open over ravines   tempests
futures   you sortof said a lot of things
    til you whispered
so slithering
    behind you, a monster!
was it your face floating sideways

on the disinfected window
or the other swollen patient
flicking his butt facing North
    I raced
with my eyes alone
above the astroturf   gutted
    sharped   nauseous
still smiling just for you
    trying to hold up your shape

afterwards   your mother delivered
a perfect sweet tart
chewing it without you
    like sand   her and I kept talking
about the end of fall   the tree in the yard
was heavy with fruit

DUNE

I can't remember if I like men or women
                    attempting a sentence on a bench
                        by the greatest dune
                              in Europe
But her lips
        we should recall
                and her iridescent skin
                        Seashell
we both wanted
        to crack open
                for the song
                      we knew hid there
I wanted
        to steal
                You wanted
                      to hear
I set you up
        I made you believe

I can't remember
        is a furry ball
                peeking out of your throat
                      thick with a world
of meds
        I still see her
                arms crossed
                      razor-mouthed

Regardless you sunk
        and now you forgot
                that time
                        and the rest

I can hardly retell
        if I even like
                at all
                        finally drops

as you grasp
        a handful
                from the greatest dune
                      in Europe

V.

I will tell you what I see
    between us a river
we all look at each other
transparent   yearning   wristwatched
we stand robbed
on our shores
someone signals to the ground
I step in like a bride

Underneath
everyone is there
I will tell you what I want
    I never thought
we could get along so well
in slo-mo   bullets
are caught with one finger
your screams
sound like bells
red paintings   rumors
quelled

Uncles   aunts
    a shoal of kids
the table is set
    no one has died yet

from a corner door
enters my grandfather
walking his way
back from the war

You've got to dizzy yourself
to sleep   my little aunt says
to her siblings   as they shake
some thoughts off their lips

My grandmother is showing
a smile   something akin
to an eclipse   through the mist
we must stare
til we are blinded

she speaks
she tells us everything
migrating   first son
secrets   hunger
sex   daughters quick
like fishes   stone
sinking in the river
and by that   she means
    dead son(s)

she speaks
we huddle
in front of the fire
    she tells us everything
touch of frost
    fodder
    on her forehead
her mother   caring
or not caring   how she learned
French so late   how
she resented   how she deciphered
alphabet   herd
burnt   frustrated

she tells
what there was to dream of
how she dealt with the dead
how unsaying   how silence
    how the boys
continued breaking their heads

On all faces
    no mildew
only morning pearls
feelings writhing
    burrowing eyebrows

we have never been so close
our elbows touching
    without collapsing

I ask all my questions
    when do you hate us so
what happens
when the weathervane looks down
and sees the pole
on which she is standing
    headspin
in all of the men's brains
epithets   retracting cells
quiet

I can feel it coming
    you say
like an irregular tide
it climbs inmyhead
throwing like jackhammers
like wedding rice
But Underneath
    is where soft and slow
catch all angles
and your mother and I
sigh by your side   calm

All the faces
    are new
fine and unsoiled
now   a single day
    the beginning
stretched into a whole life
wristwatch   bandage
    moving mouths
talking till sunset and sunrise
nothing more than talking

Saying everything
    explaining why
the fear of falling
    makes one dive

Like a bride I let go
    I step into the stream
float or sink   words
will empty
    our family out

Stonebrother
    looks vague
at the center of the table

at the center of the lake
my mother   kneeling
her eyes impossibly full
guilt-yellow   yelled out
of her eyelids
he says nothing
    or rather
I cannot hear
his voice   or I can hear
his song

Cornerstone
sunken piece
or one of the columns
    holding this mystery
house   aquarium
gregarious   lost
    simple tasks
weighing tons
weighing nothing

How heavy
are ghosts
are shadows

Your stories adrift

      my memory a hull

to hoard away
    your muffled scores

The truth is
I can't talk with you

But in my Underneath
you're all always
    swimming

ACKNOWLEDGEMENTS

My gratitude goes to the editors of the following journals, where previous versions of these poems first appeared:

Tiny Zine Hawaii: *After A Big Family Meal*
Punch Drunk Press: *Opinel*

The poem *Keeping the Chaff and the Wheat* contains a quote from "The Collected Works of Langston Hughes: Essays on art, race, politics, and world affairs", p.525, University of Missouri Press, by Langston Hughes (2002).

My warmest thanks to Julie Hart, Thad Higa, and Alex Sewell, who spent time with this manuscript and gave me thoughtful comments. Thank you also to the Sweet Action Collective, a safe haven where I was able to hone some of these poems. Finally, I send wild thanks to my family – in particular my love and partner in crime Alex, my sister Flore, and my parents, as well as Hanne Tierney, whose example I always try to follow.

ABOUT THE AUTHOR

Marine Cornuet is a poet, translator, and arts administrator currently residing in Brooklyn, NY. *Keeping the Chaff and the Wheat* is her first chapbook. Her poems can be found in *IDK Magazine, 8-West Press, Dime Show Review*, and elsewhere. She is a member of Sweet Action, a women-led poetry collective based in Brooklyn.

www.ingramcontent.com/pod-product-compliance
Lightning Source LLC
Chambersburg PA
CBHW052105110526
44591CB00013B/2365